Introduction to th iPad and iPhone

I0004860

Typing and Editing

iOS 11 Edition

© 2017 iTandCoffee

All rights reserved. No part of this book shall be reproduced, stored in a retrieval system or transmitted by any means, electronic, mechanical, photocopying, recording, or otherwise without written permission from iTandCoffee. No patent liability is assumed with respect to the use of the information contained herein. Although every precaution has been taken in the preparation of this book, the author assumes no responsibility for any errors or omissions. Nor is any liability assumed for damages resulting from the use of the information contained herein.

Special Sales and Supply Queries

For any information about buying this title in bulk quantities, or for supply of this title for educational or fund-raising purposes, contact iTandCoffee on **1300 885 420** or email **enquiry@itandcoffee.com.au**.

iTandCoffee classes and private appointments

For queries about classes and private appointments with iTandCoffee, call **1300 885 420** or email **enquiry@itandcoffee.com.au**.

iTandCoffee operates in and around Glen Iris, Victoria in Australia.

iTandCoffee
Relax, we'll help you get iT

Introducing iTandCoffee ...

iTandCoffee is a Melbourne-based business that was founded in 2012, by IT professional Lynette Coulston.

Lynette and the staff at iTandCoffee have a passion for helping others - especially women of all ages - to enter and navigate the new, and often daunting, world of technology.

At iTandCoffee, **patience is our virtue.**

You'll find a welcoming smile, a relaxed cup of tea or coffee, and a genuine enthusiasm for helping you to gain the confidence to use and enjoy your technology.

With personalised appointments and small, friendly classes – either at our bright, comfortable, cafe-style shop in Glen Iris or at your place - we offer a brand of technology support and education that is so hard to find.

At iTandCoffee, you won't find young 'techies' who speak in a foreign language and move at a pace that leaves you floundering and 'bamboozled'!

Our focus is on helping you to use your technology in a way that enhances your personal and/or professional life – to feel more informed, organised, connected and entertained!

4

iTandCoffee
Relax, we'll help you get iT

Call on iTandCoffee for help with all sorts of technology – Apple, Windows, iCloud, Evernote, Dropbox, all sorts of other Apps (including Microsoft Office products), getting you set up on the internet, setting up a printer, and so much more.

Here are just some of the topics covered in our regular classes at iTandCoffee:

- Introduction to the iPad and iPhone
- The next step on your iPad and iPhone
- Bring your Busy Life under Control using the iPad and iPhone
- Getting to know your Mac
- Understanding and using iCloud
- An Organised Life with Evernote
- Taking and Managing photos on the iPhone and iPad
- Travel with your iPad, iPhone and other technology.
- Keeping kids safe on the iPad, iPhone and iPod Touch.
- Staying Safe Online

The iTandCoffee website (itandcoffee.com.au) offers a wide variety of resources for those brave enough to venture online to learn more: handy hints for iPad, iPhone and Mac; videos and slideshows of iTandCoffee classes; guides on a range of topics; a blog covering all sorts of topical events.

We also produce a regular Handy Hint newsletter full of information that is of interest to our clients and subscribers.

Hopefully, that gives you a bit of a picture of iTandCoffee and what we are about. Please don't hesitate to iTandCoffee on 1300 885 420 to discuss our services or to make a booking.

We hope you enjoy this guide, and find its contents informative and useful. Please feel free to offer feedback at feedback@itandcoffee.com.au.

Regards,

Lynette Coulston (iTandCoffee Owner)

Typing & Editing on the iPad and iPhone

Table of Contents

Typing & Editing on the iPad and iPhone

Table of Contents

Introduction

Your iPad and iPhone provide you with an on-screen typewriter / keyboard, as well as a host of features that allow you to undertake both basic and more sophisticated text creation and editing.

But many people are unaware of how to correct and edit their text without just 'backspacing' to delete whole chunks of text, or how to move text around without having to simply re-type.

In this guide, we look at the features of your device's on-screen keyboard, and how your iPad or iPhone can become more of a replacement for a computer or laptop, by giving you the ability to create and edit emails, documents, texts and more.

We only cover the on-screen keyboard in this guide, and how to use finger techniques to navigate and select text.

Hardware keyboards connected to your device are not covered by this guide.

Introducing the Keyboard

Your iPad's (or iPhone's) on-screen keyboard will automatically appear whenever you are on a field or in an app that requires you to type something. (If you have a separate keyboard – the iPad Pro keyboard, or a third-party keyboard connected by Bluetooth, you will not see the on-screen keyboard.)

Always remember that if you don't see the keyboard, it's just because you are not currently positioned somewhere that needs you to type. Just touch on a search field, create an email or message, or go into a note or document.

When you are in a feature or app and at a spot where you are expected to type something, you will usually see your 'alpha keyboard' first. This is the keyboard with letters and a few punctuation symbols.

To switch to the 'numeric' keyboard, touch on the '123' key. You will see that key change to show 'ABC' instead.

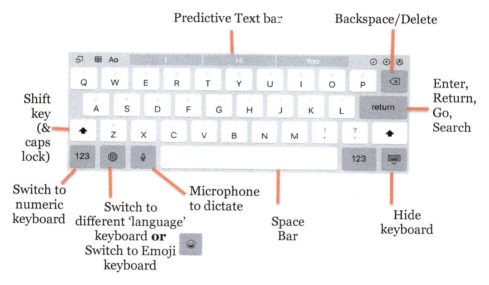

Predictive Text bar

Backspace/Delete

Enter, Return, Go, Search

Shift key (& caps lock)

Switch to numeric keyboard

Switch to different 'language' keyboard **or** Switch to Emoji keyboard

Microphone to dictate

Space Bar

Hide keyboard

To switch back to your 'alpha' keyboard, just touch on the 'ABC' key.

9

Introducing the Keyboard

There is also a third keyboard with some other symbols.

You can get to this by touching the '#+=' key from the 'numeric' keyboard.

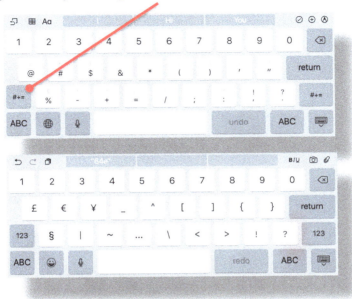

Once you have finished with this keyboard, press the **ABC** key to return to the 'alpha' keyboard, or the **123** key to return to the 'numeric' keyboard.

Hiding the keyboard

If you ever find that the keyboard is obscuring your view of something on the screen, you can get rid of it temporarily.

This can be done by touching the 'hide keyboard' button on the bottom right of the keyboard.

To get the keyboard back, once again touch any field or area on the screen that needs text entered.

Quick Access to Numbers and Symbols

With the latest iOS update, some handy quick access features have been added to the keyboard.

Both the 'alpha' and 'numeric' keyboards display additional numbers and symbols above the primary key – smaller, greyed numbers and symbols. (In the example shown on the right, the Y symbol has a 6 shown above it.)

This allows for the keys located on other keyboards to be accessed without having to switch keyboards.

To type the greyed number or symbol, simply swipe down on the key instead of tapping the key.

In the below example, dragging down on the Y key will insert a 6 instead of a Y.

On the numeric keyboard, you will notice that there are secondary keys on many of the symbol keys. These are accessed in the same way as described above.

Typing Capital Letters

Your keyboard shows upper/lowercase letters

Your device's keyboard keys will always show whether you are in 'uppercase' or 'lowercase' mode. If the next letter you type is going to be a lowercase letter, the keyboard will show lowercase letters. If the next letter you type is going to be an uppercase letter, the keyboard will show uppercase letters.

Typing a single uppercase letter

To type a letter in uppercase when your keyboard is currently showing lowercase letters, tap the **Shift** key before tapping a letter. The key's arrow will become solid black with a white background and your keyboard will show uppercase letters.

Once your letter has been typed, your 'shift' key will change back to its original state (dark grey background), indicating that your next letter will be lowercase – also indicated by the lowercase letters showing on your keyboard.

(If you keyboard is showing uppercase letters, and you wish to type a lowercase letter, tap the **Shift** key to switch to lowercase.)

Typing a series of capital letters (caps lock)

To type several capital letters consecutively, touch the **Shift** key twice in quick succession to lock your caps.

The appearance of the button when it is in 'caps lock' mode is similar to the Shift mode shown above – except it has a line underneath the arrow to indicate Caps Lock (and the letter keys on the keyboard will show uppercase letters).

Tap the **Shift** key once again to turn off Caps Lock and return to lowercase mode.

The Predictive Text Bar

The Predictive Text Bar was first introduced to the iPad and iPhone in iOS 8.

Its purpose is to assist you with your typing, by presenting - when you first start typing a word – 3 suggestions for the word that you are typing.

If you see the word you want displayed in the Predictive Text bar, just tap on it to complete your word. This can save a lot of typing!

If you misspell a word, the middle word in the predictive text bar will replace the misspelt word when you hit the **Space Bar**. You will notice that your 'misspelt' word is the left word in the Predictive Text bar.

If you actually want to keep the original spelling (and not have your word replaced by the 'correction'), just tap the word on the left in the bar.

Your Predictive Text will get smarter over time, as iOS sees patterns in what you type, and words or phrases that you use frequently.

If you don't see a **Predictive Test** bar (as shown in the right-hand image below), it may be turned 'off'.

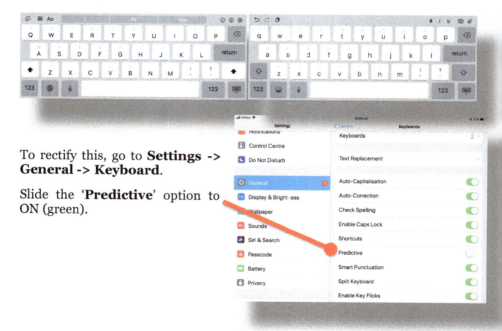

To rectify this, go to **Settings -> General -> Keyboard**.

Slide the '**Predictive**' option to ON (green).

Options on top of keyboard

On the iPad (and on the Plus versions of the iPhone when in 'landscape' orientation), you may notice some symbols that appear to the left and right of the **Predictive Text** bar. These symbols vary depending on the app that you are using, the device you are using, and where you are typing within that app.

While we won't cover these options in detail as part of this guide (and instead cover them in guides about the specific apps), here are a couple of examples of these symbols for the **Notes** and **Mail** apps (as shown on an iPad Mini).

The below image shows the symbols that you see when looking at the **Notes** app on the iPad Mini. Touch on each of these symbols to see the options available or to activate that option.

The below image shows the symbols that appear when you are typing in the body of a message while in the **Mail** app on the iPad.

Split, Merge, Dock and Undock

If you like to 'thumb-type' on your iPad using both hands, you have an option to 'split' and 'undock' your keyboard to make this easier.

To split, or dock your keyboard:

- Touch and hold the **Keyboard** key (lower right corner of keyboard)

- Slide your finger up to the **Split** option and let go to select this option

To put the keyboard back where it belongs.

- Touch and hold the keyboard symbol and slide up to the **Dock and Merge,** then let go to select that option.

Change Font Size and Appearance

If you find that the text on your iPad or iPhone is too small or too faint, you can easily adjust the font sizing and how 'bold' it appears.

Make text larger and bolder

Go to **Settings -> Display & Brightness**.

The **Text Size** and the **Bold Text** options can be found here.

Tap **Text Size**, then adjust the **Text Size** slider to your preferred size.

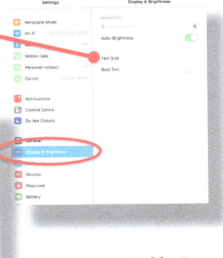

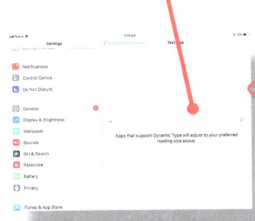

Turning on **Bold Text** option will require that your device does a restart.

Making the text size even larger

For people that have eyesight issues, it can be necessary to make the font size REALLY large.

This achieved from an area in **Settings** called **Accessibility**, which is found in the **General** area of **Settings**.

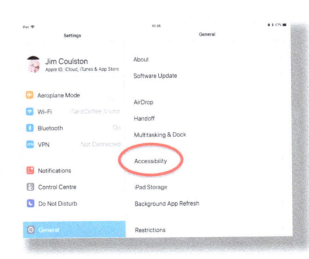

Change Font Size and Appearance

Tap the **Larger Tex**t option in the **VISION** area of Accessibility.

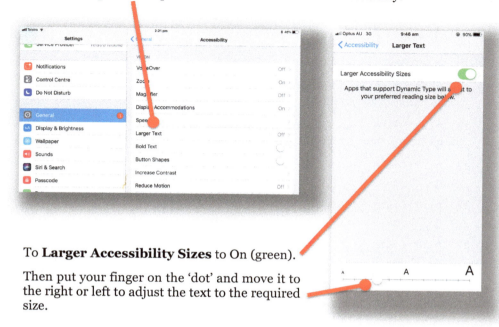

To **Larger Accessibility Sizes** to On (green).

Then put your finger on the 'dot' and move it to the right or left to adjust the text to the required size.

Some other options to assist with visibility

There are a few other options in the Vision area of the **Accessibility** menu, to **Increase Contrast** (to **Reduce** Transparency and **Darken Colours)** and put **Button Shapes** around options.

The image on the right shows the normal colour for the Albums option in Photos;

The image on the right shows the impact of turning on **Darken Colours**;

The image on the right shows what the same option looks like with **Button Shapes** turned on.

Play with these options if you find that colours and shapes are too faint or hard to make out.

Navigating text

Your iPad and iPhone has some clever features that make it relatively easy (with a bit of practice!) to navigate your text and find a position in your text, so that you can then do some deletion, editing, copying and several other things!

Tap to set your cursor position

You can try just tapping on the screen (single tap) at the position where you want the cursor to be positioned. This often works really well, but it can be easy to 'miss the mark' especially, say, when you want to correct an error in your typing of a website address.

Navigate using Insertion Point Method

So here is another way of setting your cursor's position – it's called the **Insertion Point Method**.

1. Hold your finger on the screen until a little magnifying glass appears above your finger.

2. Without lifting your finger, move it **over the top of text** (not above or below) to the point in the text where insertion or deletion is required. Make sure your finger is covering the line of text – otherwise it won't appear in the magnifying glass.

3. Take your finger off the screen.

4. Your 'cursor' (i.e. the line that shows your current text position) will be left at the point where you lifted your finger.

Navigating Text

Navigate using the Trackpad on the iPad

Your iPad offers a feature familiar to Macbook and PC users, known as the trackpad.

Touching with two fingers on the keyboard causes the keyboard to go into Trackpad mode. The keys will go blank.

Keep the two fingers on the keyboard and drag the cursor to the required position in your text.

This can sometimes be easier than using other methods for positioning the cursor, but takes a bit of practise.

Navigating using the Trackpad on the iPhone

If you are lucky enough to have one of the newer iPhones (iPhone 6S and newer), you will also have trackpad functionality built in to your iPhone's keyboard.

This trackpad is enabled in a different manner to that which applies on the iPad.

Just press a bit harder than usual on the keyboard (ie use 'force touch'), and you will see your keyboard turn into a trackpad.

Slide your finger around while maintaining the slight pressure to move the cursor around and find your position.

Deleting text

To delete the text to the left of where the cursor is positioned, just use the **backspace/delete** key on the keyboard:

1. Tap once to delete the letter to the <u>left</u> of selected point.

2. Hold down the backspace/delete key to 'walk' backwards (i.e. delete multiple letters).

3. Keep holding it down and it will begin to delete whole words, then sentences, then full paragraphs of text.

Selecting text

Sometimes, it is necessary to select an area of text – a single word, several words, an entire paragraph, or the entire email/document – so that you can then choose to do something with it.

The options for what you can the 'do' with selected text varies by app.

To select a single word

The easiest way to select a word is to **double-tap** on the word – the selected word will appear shaded in a colour (for example blue for the Mail app, yellow for Notes). Below shows a screen shot from the Notes app.

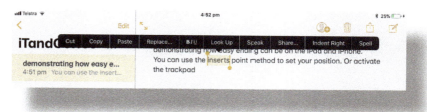

You can also use any of the methods described earlier in Navigating Text to set your cursor position, then tap on the word **Select** in the black bar that appears.

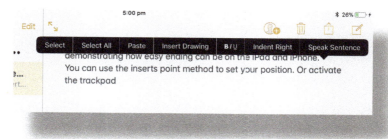

This will select the word on the left of the cursor (see below). You will also see the two dots on either side of the word, which are known as 'handles'.

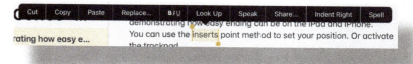

These 'handles' can be 'stretched out' to select more text.

Selecting Text

To select more than one word

For times where you need to select more than a single word, there are a couple of options.

To select all the text in the message, email or document ...

Touch and hold anywhere on the screen until you see the magnifying glass, then let go. You will see a black bar appear above or below the 'cursor'

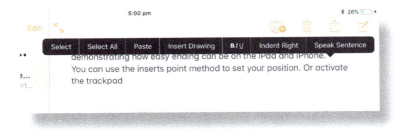

Touch on **Select All** to select all the text in the applicable area (for example, all the text in the Note, all the text in the body of the email, all the text in the search bar in which you are typing). All the selected text will have a coloured background.

To select just some of the text in the message, email or document ...

- Try to position your cursor near the text that needs to be selected, then tap on **Select** in the black bar (instead of **Select All**).

OR alternatively

- Just double tap on a word that is in (or near) the area that you want to select.

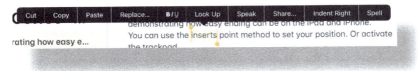

Regardless of which of these you choose, you will end up with some selected text with a coloured background, with dots on either end.

The dots are 'handles' that you can touch on, then drag to select the text you need.

Selecting Text

- Touch and hold on the left-hand dot, and drag it leftwards and/or upwards to select text on the left and/or above the selected text.

- Touch and hold on the right-hand dot, and drag it rightwards and/or downwards to select text on the right and/or below the selected text.

- When you 'let go', you will see the black bar with options appear above the text that has been selected, which will be shaded with a colour.

Using the iPad Trackpad to Select Text

If you wish to select some text, use the trackpad (or another method) to set your cursor position (as described earlier).

Once you have your position (and you can release your two fingers if you used the Trackpad to do this positioning), touch and hold again with two fingers.

This time, let your two fingers rest for a bit longer until you see the 'edit mode' (with the two dots) appear around some of the nearby text.

Drag your two fingers left or right over the trackpad until you have selected the required text.

Using the iPhone Trackpad to Select Text

Use your iPhone's trackpad to set your cursor position (as described earlier).

To select an area of text, release the pressure just slightly – then drag across the area of text that you require.

It takes a bit of getting used to, but works very well once you master the technique!

Options for your selected text -
the Black Bar

Once you have some text selected (using any of the methods described above), you can do several things with it.

The options that you see in the black bar will depend on which app you are using, where you are positioned in that app and whether you have selected a single word or several words.

Below shows the bar that appears when you select an area of text in Notes.

Below shows the bar that appears when you select text in the body of the Mail app (which extends by tapping the ▶ symbol on the right)

Here are just some of the options you may see. Tap to select the required option in the bar.

1. **Cut** – this means removing the text from its current spot, but leaving it in your iPad or iPhone's memory so that you can go somewhere else and choose to 'Paste' it.

2. **Copy** – this means leaving the text where it is, but taking a copy of the selected text and putting it into your iPad or iPhone's memory so that you can, again, go somewhere else and 'paste' it.

3. **Insert Photo or Video** – this will allow you to choose a photo from your Photos app to insert at the point you have selected. If you have some text selected, the photo will replace the highlighted text.

4. **Add Attachment** – to add a file.

5. **Insert Drawing** – to add a drawing.

6. **Replace** offers suggestions of similar words which you might have meant instead of the word selected.

7. **Look Up** – find a dictionary meaning for the word selected.

8. **B/U** - change the formatting of the selected text to make it bold, italics, and/or underline it,

9. **Quote** - change the indent or 'Quote Level' of the selected text.

10. **Speak** - You can even get your device to 'Speak' the selected text.

    (Go to **Settings -> General -> Accessibility -> Speech** and turn ON '**Speak Selection**'. The **Speaking Rate** can be adjusted from that Accessibility option.)

Cutting, copying, pasting

There will be times when it is necessary to select some text and either copy it to somewhere else, or remove it and move it to elsewhere.

Once you have your text selected, it's easy to achieve both. The following instructions are universal to iOS versions.

1. Select the applicable text (refer previous section), so that the black menu bar is showing and the text is shaded.

2. Touch **Copy** or **Cut** from the black menu bar – it you chose **Cut**, the selected text will disappear.

3. If you want to put the text in a different App, switch to place where the 'copied' or 'cut' text is to be inserted.

4. Select a new insertion point using the technique described earlier in 'Navigating Text' – you need to touch and hold (then let go) on place where text is to be inserted, so that the black bar with the menu options pops up (or use your device's trackpad to set the position).

5. Choose **Paste** to insert the previously cut/copied text at the point you have selected.

There is an alternative to using the black bar's options on those devices that have additional symbols at the top left and right of the keyboard.

Normally, you will see this symbol at the top left. ↰

However, whenever you select some text (ie whenever there is some shaded text, the top left symbol changes to ✄↰

Tap on this symbol to uncover the cut, copy and paste options.

Use these if you prefer them to the 'black bar' options.

✄   ⬚   ⬚

cut   copy   paste

Oops – I didn't mean to do that!

The ability to select a large 'chunk' of text and delete it is great, but what if you accidentally delete instead of copy that big chunk of text!

Don't worry – you can undo mistakes like this in a couple of ways.

Shake to undo

Yes, you can just **shake** your iPad or iPhone to undo the last made change or deletion.

The options 'Undo' and 'Cancel' will appear on the screen, and the heading above these options will show what action you are going to be 'undoing'.

Just touch the blue **Undo** option to complete the 'undo.

Shake again, and you will see the **Redo** option

Or use the 'undo' symbol at top of iPad keyboard

I'm not a huge fan of shaking my iPad, so prefer an alternative way of 'undoing'.

On the top left of the iPad keyboard, you will see a symbol that allows you to choose to 'undo' something you typed, deleted, formatted and more.

(You may need to first tap the ↶ symbol to reveal the ↶ option.)

Tap the ↶ to undo the last change – tap again to undo the change before that (and before that, etc.).

Did you 'undo' too much?!

If you **undo** too much, you can choose the **redo** ↷ symbol on the iPad, which is to the right of the **undo** symbol. This will 'undo your undo'!

Formatting your text

Depending on the app in which you are working when performing your selection and text editing, you may have some formatting options available in the black menu bar.

To make the selected text bold, italics or underlined in the Mail App.

1. Select a word by double tapping

2. *OR* select several words using the method described earlier.

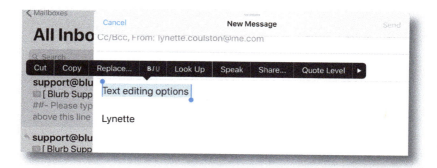

3. Touch on the **B*I*U** option on the black menu bar.

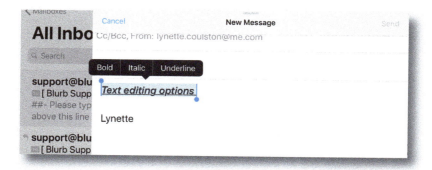

4. Select the required option.

If you are on your iPhone, you may not see the **B*I*U** option when the black bar first appears.

   Just touch on the ▶ symbol on the right-hand side of the black bar to see the **B*I*U** option (as well as some other options).

In the Notes app, you will have other text formatting options that can be uncovered by tapping on symbols at the top left and right of the keyboard.

Word definitions and suggestions

To find a word definition, synonyms or spelling corrections...

1. Select a word by double tapping on it.

2. If you are on a phone, you may need to choose the ▷ arrow on right to see other options

3. Touch on the **Replace** option to see similar words or correction.

4. Touch on the required word to replace the selected word.

5. Touch on the **Look Up** option to see a definition of the selected word – this is only available if a single word is selected, and if the word is in device's dictionary.

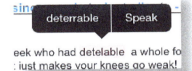

Text Replacements

What are Text Replacements?

Text Replacements are a great way of saving yourself from typing common words and phrases in full – which can be a great time saver for those frequently uses words, terms and phrases.

By defining a Text Replacement, for a phrase, you only need to type a few letters - and your device will be able to automatically translate this 'code' into to the longer phrase!

For example

- 'sys' = 'see you soon'
- 'omw' = 'on my way'
- 'eitc' = enquiry@itandcoffee.com.au

Create as many as you like! I use these shortcuts most for my email addresses – I just type in three or four letters, and a full email address appears.

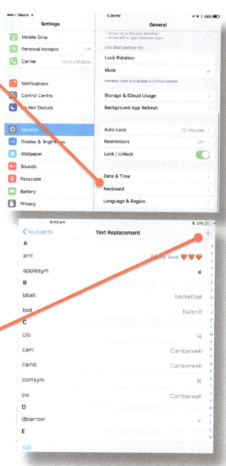

1. Go to **Settings -> General -> Keyboard**.

2. Touch on **Text Replacement**.

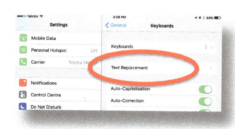

3. You will see the list of existing shortcuts (if there are any).

4. To create a new Shortcut, touch the '+' symbol at top right.

Text Replacements

5. Type in the **Phrase** first. It can even include emojis!

6. Then type in a shortcut 'code' for this phrase - one that you are likely to remember in future.

7. When finished, select Save (top right).

Now, when you are typing an email, text, or in a field on a form, you can just type in the shortcut and the replacement text will appear above it.

For example, if I type **aml** then a space, my phrase **All my love** 💜💜💜 will be automatically replace **aml**.

When I type **aml**, the replacement text appears in the predictive text bar, showing what the replacement will be.

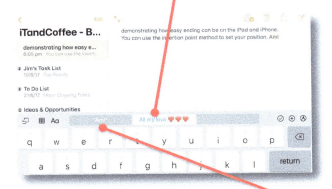

If I don't want that text replacement, I must tap the left-hand word in the predictive text bar, to confirm that I instead want to type **Aml**.

Are you a fan of Emojis?

Do you love smiley faces in texts and emails, but wondered how you can get them on your iPad and iPhone?

These little pictures are called Emojis!

You get access to them by adding the 'Emoji keyboard' to your device. This will then give you access to whole variety of little pictures that you can use when you are creating texts and emails – and everywhere else.

If you don't already have it, you can 'install' your Emoji keyboard from **Settings**.

1. Go to **Settings > General > Keyboard**.

2. Touch **Keyboards.**

3. Touch **Add New Keyboard**

4. Find the Emoji keyboard in the list displayed (which is alphabetical), and touch on it.

5. The Emoji keyboard will then be added to your list of available Keyboards.

As you will have seen when selecting the Emoji keyboard, there are keyboards for lots of different languages – add whatever language/s you need by following the same process.

Are you a fan of Emojis?

So, now that the Emoji keyboard is installed, how do you access it when you are typing?

It's easy! Just touch on the keyboard key with 'globe' symbol or the 'smiley face symbol. This key is to the left of the space bar, near the 'numeric keyboard' key.

(You will see the globe if you have more than one additional keyboard enabled on your device.)

Tapping this key will replace the standard keyboard with the Emoji keyboard.

Touch on any keys on this keyboard to insert that picture into your message or document.

Choose from the different options along to bottom to see different types of Emoji's. Swipe from right to left and left to right to see the variety of Emoji's.

To return to the standard keyboard, touch on **ABC** at bottom left (or, if you see it, the 'Globe' key) to return to the standard keyboard.

Discovering hidden keys

Many letter, punctuation and symbol keys on the iPad/iPhone keyboard have 'hidden' keys behind them.

If you hold your finger on a particular key any hidden keys will appear (if there are any).

For example, hidden behind the '$' key is other currency symbols. Hidden behind the zero key is the 'degree' symbol º.

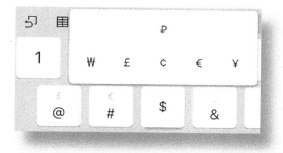

To select one of the hidden keys ...

Leave your finger on the screen and slide it to the required key, then simply take your finger off.

Why not see what other keys you can find hidden on your keyboard?

Keyboard Settings

There are a few more settings for your Keyboard that you may want to look at.

If you don't like a particular feature (for example, auto-correction), you can turn off the associated keyboard feature.

These are all available in **Settings -> General ->Keyboard**. These settings are designed to help you while you type. Here are some of them.

Auto-Capitalisation

If enabled, the first word of every sentence is capitalised for you.

Auto-Correction

If this setting is on, any errors you make while typing will be automatically corrected and your device will also make suggestions for you in the predictive text bar.

Check Spelling

If this setting is on, your iPad will look for spelling errors and underline them in red.

Enable Caps Lock

If enabled, you can tap the Shift twice to set Caps Lock.

"." Shortcut option

If enabled, entering two spaces when you are typing will insert '.' – just tap the space key twice to end a sentence and have a '.' added for you.

But really, why bother typing at all?

Dictate your words instead of typing

If your iPad or iPhone is one of the newer ones that has a voice-to-text feature, you can pretty much avoid typing completely – as long as you learn how to speak clearly and learn how to add punctuation with words.

Touch on the 'microphone' bottom on the left of the space bar.

If this is the first time that you have touched that key, you will be asked if you wish to 'enable dictation'. You will need to agree to do this.

When you tap the microphone key, you will hear a short beep and the keyboard will disappear, replaced by a bar like that below. Just speak slowly and clearly.

When you are finished, touch the small microphone at the bottom

Just wait a moment, and you will then see the text that has been 'heard' by your device inserted into your message or document. Hopefully it closely resembles what you said! If you want to record more words, tap the microphone again.

But really, why bother typing at all?

Otherwise, tap the small keyboard symbol at bottom right to bring back the keyboard.

Phrases for punctuation and formatting

To add punctuation when dictating your text, just say the words 'full stop' or 'comma' at the points where they need to be inserted.

Below is a list of phrases to use to add your punctuation and formatting when dictating.

   new line - To add a new line of text (carriage return)

   new paragraph - To start a new paragraph

   cap - To capitalize the next letter of the next word

   caps on/off - To capitalize the first letter of every word in a section

   all caps - To capital all letters in the next word

   all caps on/off - Capital all letters in next section of text

   no caps - Make all of the next letters in the next word lower case

   no caps on/off - Make all next letters in next section lower case

   space bar - Prevent hyphenation from occurring in a normally hyphenated word

   no space - Prevent a space between two words

   no space on/off - Prevent space in a section of text

   period or *full stop* - Place a period at the end of a sentence

   dot - Places a dot (period) within text, but no space after

   ellipsis - Places an ellipse (...) in the next space

   comma - Places a comma at the location of the cursor

   quote - Places a quotation mark at the cursor

   apostrophe - Places an apostrophe at the cursor

   exclamation point - Places an exclamation point at the cursor

But I don't have a microphone key

If you find that your device's keyboard is missing the microphone key, this can be fixed by turning on the **Enable Dictation** option in

   Settings -> General- > Keyboard

Other Guides in the **Introduction to the iPad and iPhone** Series

* **A Guided Tour of your iPad and iPhone**
* **Taking Photos and Videos**
* **Viewing and Managing Photos and Videos**
* **Keeping in Touch: The Mail App**
* **Keeping in Touch: The Phone App**
* **Exploring the Internet on Safari**
* **Getting Organised: The Calendar App**
* **Let's Go Shopping – Exploring the Stores**
* **Discovering iBooks**
* **Getting Connected**

www.ingramcontent.com/pod-product-compliance
Lightning Source LLC
Chambersburg PA
CBHW041635050326
40689CB00024B/4971